IMAGES OF ENGLAND

COVENTRY

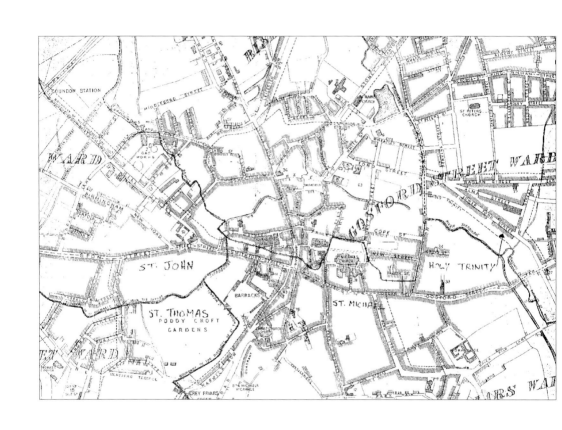

IMAGES OF ENGLAND

COVENTRY

GEOFF BARWICK

TEMPUS

Frontispiece: Central Coventry from an 1879 survey map. *(Courtesy of Coventry City Libraries and Information Services.)*

First published 2005

Tempus Publishing Limited
The Mill, Brimscombe Port,
Stroud, Gloucestershire, GL5 2QG
www.tempus-publishing.com

British Library Cataloguing in Publication Data.
A catalogue record for this book is available from the British Library.

ISBN 0 7524 3533 7
Typesetting and origination by Tempus Publishing Limited.
Printed in Great Britain.

Contents

	Acknowledgements	6
	Introduction	7
one	Around the City	9
two	Coventry Citizens	43
three	The Watch Trade	73
four	Schooldays	83
five	At Work and Play	91
six	Transport	107

Acknowledgements

The author would like to thank the Coventry Family History Society members, friends and organisations that have contributed their photographs and illustrations – this book would not have been possible without their generosity:

Frank Bagley, Judith Bramwell, Peter Cooke, Coventry City Libraries and Information Services, Coventry Record Office, Coventry and Warwickshire Chamber of Commerce, Coventry Watch Museum Project, Win Dolphin, Sheila Duffy, Kay Dunkley, Joyce Franklin, John Gibberd, Carol Griffiths, Jeromy Hassell, the Horner Family, John Hyde, Mavis Miles, Freda Nicholson, Doris Pails, Jack Siddle, Muriel Sinclair, Vic Terry, Edna Ward, Stephen Watkinson.

Special thanks to William Dunn and his committee for allowing access to the Earlsdon Society collection, Coventry artist Graham Bosworth for his Jaguar montage that closes the book and to Rachel and Peter Cooke for advice on layout and captions.

All efforts were made to obtain permission to use the material in this book but, where copyright has not been traced, apologies are given.

Introduction

The history of Coventry is well recorded, from the early settlement around the confluence of its main water courses – the Radford Brook and River Sherbourne – through to the near demise of its main industrial life at the end of the twentieth century. The prosperity of the Earl Leofric/Lady Godiva period was the factor which raised Coventry above the surrounding villages and hamlets to its prominence. Approaching the mediaeval walled city must have presented the traveller with a wondrous view, certainly from higher ground, and it is still possible to see Holy Trinity church from Corley. The city wall had twelve gates spaced around it; illustrations of five, courtesy of Coventry City Libraries and Information Services, have been used for the chapter title pages.

Although it is difficult to visualise now, for many years the Sherbourne was a major factor in the city's growth and wealth. That growth, particularly in the twentieth century, certainly helped to make the Sherbourne the trickle it is today. The weaving and dyeing industry, for which the city was famous for many years, was built on the water supply from the river. As well as supplying all the dyeworks, there were also mills along its course as it wound through the city and on to its junction with the Sowe. On occasions of heavy rainfall the river flooded quite readily, leaving Spon End, Spon Street and Pool Meadow under water. This is recorded as early as 1607.

Watchmaking, established in the eighteenth century, expanded in the nineteenth century as the weaving industry waned and from the 1850s was the major employer of people in the city. As the weaving industry had made some businessmen rich, so did the watch industry. However, these men saw to it that the city benefited from their wealth through endowments, gifts and trusts; this practice being carried on by later businessmen. They built new factories with houses nearby for their workforces.

In the established manner, the watch trade peaked and began to decline in the face of overseas competition. It was replaced by the manufacture of cycles, which progressed into the motorcycle and motor car industry. This led to a further demand for workers to man the factories, houses for their families and to the enlarging of the machine tool industry that was established in the city. The period just before and just after the Second World War provided another surge in these industries and the city expanded its area dramatically to its present size.

The memory of the watch trade is being kept alive by the 'Coventry Watch Museum Project Ltd' under the chairmanship of Paul Shufflebotham, a direct descendant of a nineteenth-century watch manufacturer. The Project has purchased three cottages behind the Shakespeare Inn, Spon Street. These were part of Court No. 7 which used to house watch trade families.

As industries changed, so did the people. The various Coventry censuses show that when weaving was the main industry many workers moved from Lancashire to work in the city. The watch trade similarly attracted workers from Middlesex and Lancashire, notably from Clerkenwell and Prescot respectively. The cycle and motor industries brought people not only from the surrounding villages of Warwickshire and neighbouring counties, but also from overseas. This was not new to the city though – a look at the 1861 census reveals Coventry residents born in America, Russia, France, the West Indies, the East Indies and Prussia to name but a few. Also, from the early days Coventry ran an apprentice scheme, which brought young people into the city. However, by the middle of the eighteenth century, because 'freemen' had the right to vote, the system was grossly abused, with the status being purchased in large numbers to 'rig' elections. The scheme was terminated, a new one started and rigid rules applied ensuring that 'freeman' status could only be gained by serving a full apprenticeship within the city. Records were kept of the new scheme from 1781 and continue today.

With the invention of photography in the nineteenth century we begin to have a visual record of people, places and life in Coventry. These early images are now valued not only for their age but also for the social story they tell, enabling us more to appreciate the living conditions and hardships of bygone eras. The illustrations in this volume are mainly from the collections of members of the Coventry Family History Society and as such there tends to be more photographs of people than places, but they reflect the full range of life in the city from the well-off to the ordinary. I particularly like the image on page 59 of the young girls in Meadow Street – they seem to symbolise the old saying 'We haven't got much, but we do see life'. A number of the group photographs show buildings in the background, some still there and recognisable, others vastly changed or long gone. I have tried to present a cross section of city life, keeping well-known photographs to the absolute minimum and, apart from a few postcard views, most of the illustrations have not previously been seen in a general publication.

Geoff Barwick
March 2005

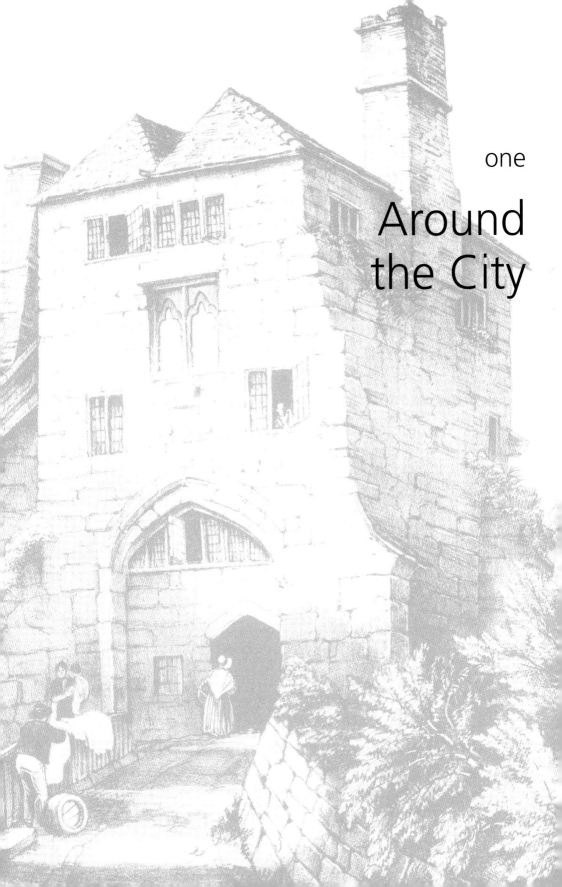

one

Around
the City

A postcard from 1911 depicting the 'Lady Godiva' theme. 1911 was a year of a Godiva Procession, an event which occurred every four years.

Gosford Green, c. 1910. St Margaret's church on Ball Hill has not been hidden behind the railway embankment at this date. The young boy beside the lamp-post looks intrigued by the unusual sight of a photographer!

The horse trough in Binley Road, July 1980. The inscription reads: 'Metropolitan Drinking Fountain & Cattle Trough Association'. In its heyday it would largely have been used by horses, but as the name suggests would also have been used by cattle. Dickens' *Dictionary of London* (1879) reported that 'the Metropolitan Drinking Fountain and Cattle Trough Association has erected and is now maintaining nearly 800 fountains and troughs, at which an enormous quantity of water is consumed daily. It is estimated that 300,000 people take advantage of the fountains on a summer's day, and a single trough has supplied the wants of 1,800 horses in one period of twenty-four hours'.

A postcard view of the picturesque Primrose Hill Park in 1912.

An aerial view of the Coventry rail station complex in 1972, with Warwick Road in the foreground and Cheylesmore spread either side of the line to Leamington Spa.

Opposite above: A postcard showing St Osburg's church in Hill Street, *c.* 1908.

Opposite below: The nave and font of St Thomas' church. The church was built in the Butts with the vicarage alongside, the cost being partly met by a grant from the Church Building Commission. It was consecrated in 1849. Both the church and the vicarage were demolished in 1976.

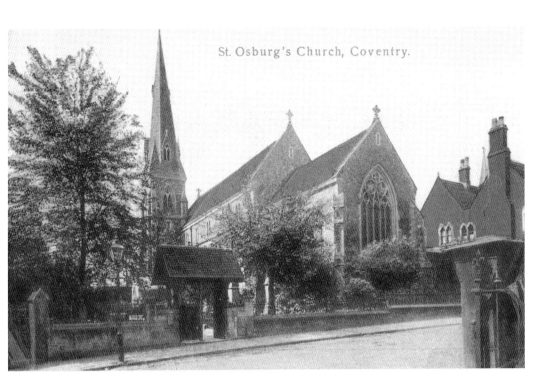

St. Osburg's Church, Coventry.

Above: This view of part of the Radford Road probably dates from around 1905. Although there are wide pavements on either side, a pram is being pushed along the road.

Below: A view down Browning Road shortly after it was built, around 1934. This photograph was found behind a fireplace in one of the houses.

Coat of Arms Bridge,
Coventry.

Above and below: Coat of Arms Bridge Road viewed from the Baginton Road side and, below, from the Green Lane side. Both are pastoral scenes taken when Styvechale was a hamlet well outside Coventry. The bridge was built in 1844. Its name is the result of a clash four years earlier between railway owners who wished to build a bridge and the local landowners who resisted it. Finally in 1842 Mr Gregory Hood agreed to sell the necessary land to the railway, but only on the condition that his family coat of arms would appear prominently on the resulting bridge.

Entrance to Court No. 1 in Thomas Street between houses Nos 13-14. This photograph was taken in 1959 when the houses were awaiting demolition to make way for the ring road development.

Right and below: Court No. 1, Thomas Street. The courts were floored with 'engineering blue' bricks. This drain gully is offset as there were houses only on one side, seven in all.

Above: Demolition work is in progress in Albion Street, *c.* 1959. It must have been thirsty work, so the Globe Tavern on the left may have been the last to be pulled down. Thomas Street is to the right.

Left: Swanswell Gate, also known as the Priory Gate, which was built in 1461. It is one of only two of the original twelve city gates which is still standing. Only a small building remains at the bottom of Lady Herbert's Garden. The upper floor has been removed and the top castellated.

Spon End, with transport and people in an apparently haphazard mix. The Malt Shovel, one of Coventry's oldest pubs, dating originally from the mid-eighteenth century, is on the right, just beyond the horse and cart by the kerb. The road is still a busy thoroughfare today.

Above and below: These views of old Coventry on a souvenir postcard from 1908 were also issued as separate postcards. The message on the back states the writer's intention to send postcards with views of Coventry, to remind the recipient of home.

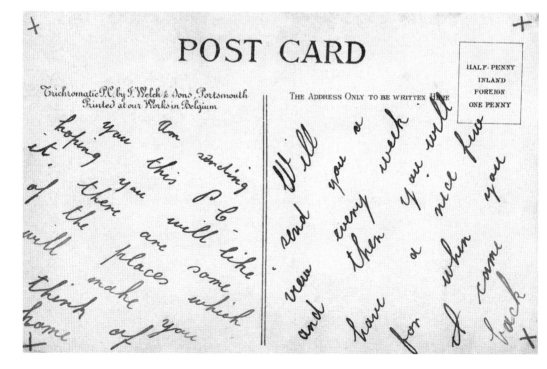

Above: On the corner of Earlsdon Avenue North and Newcombe Road, F.E. Ayre's grocery stores made full use of the available wall space to advertise products such as Colman's mustard and Cadbury's cocoa, making it difficult to see the road nameplate, *c.* 1914.

Below: Mr Murray, the original owner of this well-known shop at 46 Earlsdon Street, in 1924.

From a painting of High Street in 1932 by local artist C.S. Gibberd. Note that the entrance to Anslows is in Hay Lane, later to be moved to the corner of the building where it is today. John Anslow's furniture shop served Coventry people for many years before being bought by Waring & Gillow, the well-known furniture makers. They sold the premises to the company that converted them into a pub/bar.

Above: Radford Road looking towards the city from the railway bridge, with Beaumont, Chemist on the left.

Right: The outer gateway and house of the old Whitefriars Monastery has been used as a toy museum for some years. In the sixteenth century Queen Elizabeth addressed the people of Coventry from a window in the monastery. The cloister building was subsequently used as a workhouse refuge.

Spon End.
Coventry.
Ernest. G. Bates

The River Sherbourne from Spon End Bridge, sketched in the 1950s by local artist Ernest G. Bates. This unusual viewpoint, incorporating the backs of houses in Spon End, is still substantially the same today.

The old Barras Green Working Men's Club on the corner of Coventry Street, with the Red House Inn to the right.

A group of smartly-dressed children pose for the camera outside Jesson House (No. 2 White Street). Previously the residence of photographer Richard Green, his shop is on the right. In 1909 it became the headquarters of the Coventry branch of the newly renamed Social Democratic Party.

This photographic montage shows part of Stoke Heath viewed from the top of Alpha House. At the bottom right is the new Barras Green WMC frontage.

Opposite above: This department store name was on a glass plate attached to the building in Corporation Street, opposite the old gas showrooms site.

Opposite below: The view from the cathedral tower past Holy Trinity church – one of the large buildings in the city to escape destruction during the bombing of the Second World War – showing part of the city centre being cleared for rebuilding, *c.* 1947.

Above: The area between Much Park Street and the Gaumont buildings almost cleared for the Lanchester College extension around 1960. Behind the Gaumont block on the left can be seen the temporary building which housed Marks & Spencer after the war.

Right: This postcard shows a newly opened sweet shop in Earlsdon Avenue in 1921, after a conversion to the frontage and front room/entrance hall. The selection in the window certainly looks a tempting prospect!

Opposite, above and below: The original City Arms (Ma Cooper's) in Earlsdon Street. The upper photograph shows the redoubtable Mrs Cooper at the front, while the lower image shows the Chambers family and two barmaids, *c.* 1930. The present City Arms was built in 1931.

Little Butcher Row, so named because of the occupation of many of its inhabitants, photographed in the early twentieth century. Together with Great Butcher Row, these buildings were demolished for the new Trinity Street area in the mid–1930s. If only Ye Olde Curiosity Shoppe was still standing, what character it would give to Coventry.

Looking down on Priory Row and Hill Top in the 1950s. Holy Trinity overspill churchyard can be seen at the top left, now converted into the sunken Priory Gardens.

Tile Hill Lane/Station Road crossroads in 1946. A petrol station still stands on the corner where Viner Bros Ltd can be seen, but today it has blocks of shops on either side.

The Acorn in Potters Green when newly built in the 1960s. It was demolished in the 1980s.

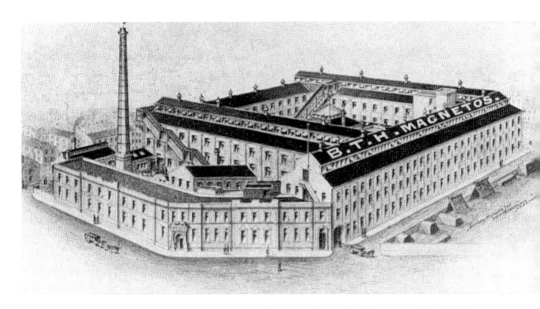

A sketch of the British Thomson-Houston Coventry Works in Lower Ford Street in 1916. Built, by Humber, in the late nineteenth century for cycle manufacture, it was taken over by the BTH Co. Ltd around 1914. All Saints Lane is on the right.

Meadow Street, with an old silk dyeworks on the left, and its junction with Trafalgar Street at the bottom, *c.* 1959.

Probably a view down Trafalgar Street with part of the old Rudge works on the left.

A view of Albany Road, c. 1935. This road was built to connect Earlsdon village to Coventry at its junction with the Butts. It was officially opened in 1899 by the Duchess of Albany.

Most of the creations in Mrs E. Bromley's millinery shop at No. 68 Albany Road appear to use feathers. Opposition to this fashion and the trading of wild plumage resulted in the formation of the RSPB in 1889.

Above and right: Two illustrations of St Michael's parish church, which became Coventry Cathedral in 1918. The earlier one above shows the original building surrounded by its extensive churchyard, the finials seen in the lower photograph were later additions. The buildings in the background of both pictures are also of interest.

THE CATHEDRAL, COVENTRY.

Above: A view of the rear of buildings in Much Park Street (see page 29) before demolition in 1970. Lea Francis Cars Ltd occupied premises on both sides of the street when they produced cars in this part of Coventry.

Left: Rover showrooms in Warwick Row, as depicted in a 1911 colour postcard celebrating the Lady Godiva Procession and the Coronation of King George V. The Meteor Works behind these extended through to Garfield Road and Queen Victoria Road.

Cook Street Gate, photographed before renovation in 1918 but after the living quarters had been removed, reducing the height. The buildings to the right were demolished and the site used for Lady Herbert's garden in 1935, this runs down to the Swanswell Gate.

Left and below: It is not surprising that Mr Thomas moved from his 1923 shop at 58 Earlsdon Street (left) to the larger premises at No. 52, shown below in this 1937 photograph.

Right: Looking up Hertford Street in the 1950s with the Empire Cinema canopy in the centre, beyond the Westminster Bank.

Below: 'The Towers' on the corner of Queens Road/Warwick Road. All of these buildings were demolished for the ring road development.

Pool Meadow bus station with the ring road construction in the background. Corporation buses were maroon with a cream stripe but there was usually one or two in the fleet that were vice versa. Two double-deck and one singe-deck versions can be seen in this photograph.

Part of the raised section of the ring road now completed. The Coventry Theatre (Hippodrome) and fire station can also be seen.

A now rare glimpse of the River Sherbourne in the city centre, exiting one of its culverts in Palmer Lane.

Cyclists tackling Gibbet Hill in this view looking towards Coventry.

Workers for A. Robinson contractors pose for a photograph during the construction of a sewer culvert for the new Cheylesmore estate in 1935.

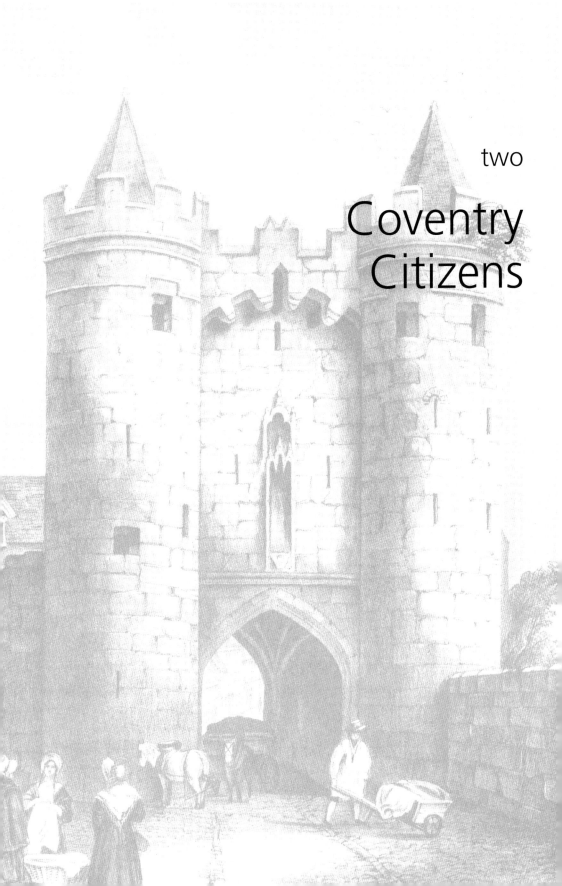

two

Coventry
Citizens

Gertrude Makepeace busy making ice cream on the back step of her home in 1930. The ice cream was sold in the family shop at No. 6 Hertford Place (below).

Right: A sketch showing Morris Engines Repair Shop personnel who were at the Gosford Street factory prior to their move to Courthouse Green in 1938.

Below: One of the male wards in Coventry Workhouse with attendant Edward Dennis (1882-1941).

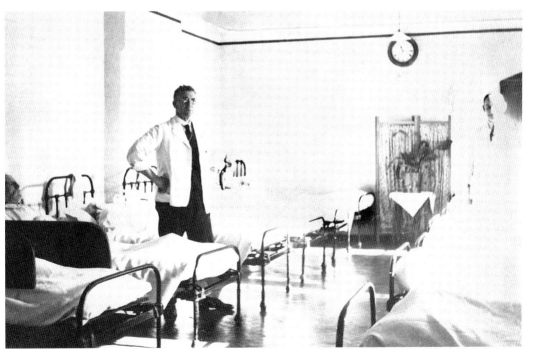

A group of workhouse residents with three attendants photographed in the workhouse grounds, possibly around 1920.

Coventry and District Master Bakers Association entry for the 1907 carnival photographed in the grounds of Robins & Powers flour mills, Wheatley Street. The 'our daily bread' lettering on the float was made of bread and the long white object on the left was a collecting bag on a pole so that people watching the procession from the upper-storey windows could contribute to the charity collection which was, and still is, always part of the day.

Right: A newspaper advert from a 1981 Coventry newspaper.

Opposite below: The wedding group of Albert Watkins and Frances Russell in 1901, They were married at All Saints church in Far Gosford Street. The Humber/ BTH factory is in the background (see page 32) with All Saints Lane between the factory and the garden wall.

These three girls and their swimming coach were proud of the trophy they had won, *c.* 1920.

Sophia Lomas, aged seven in 1861 (see page 76).

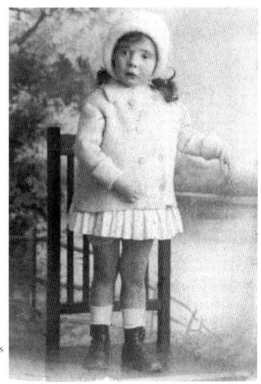

Kitty Doreen Walker (affectionately known as Dorie) of Hamilton Road, Stoke. Aged five in 1923. The photograph was taken by Gale's Studios Ltd which had offices at 10 Cross Cheaping, Coventry.

Postwoman Violet Turner wearing the ladies' uniform of 1918. The photograph was labelled 'With love, Violet, 30-3-18'.

The wedding group of Samuel Gill and Violet Simpson, 1926. Most likely photographed in Massers Yard off Aldermans Green Road.

The wedding photograph of Clarence Henry Causer and Emma Smallbun, July 1917. Clarence was born at the Malt Shovel, 93 Spon End and Emma lived at No. 96. Emma's sister Annie Elizabeth is on the right at the back.

Fred Aughton aged two years and four months in 1913. He is wearing his best clothes: a velvet suit, lace collar and buckle shoes.

Another photograph of Fred, now aged four, in a holiday photograph with his parents, Frederick and Minnie, in Blackpool.

Sarah Braunholz *née* Pugh, looking through a photograph album in the garden, *c.* 1914. Sarah was born in Much Park Street and emigrated to Queensland, Australia in 1866, joining some of her siblings who had emigrated earlier.

Left: Lieutenant Victor Goodchild, 1918. He was a pilot trainer in the Royal Flying Corps, which was formed in May 1912. He was posted to France in September 1918, contracted pneumonia and died in October 1918. He was buried in France.

Below: Outside the 'Brewer & Baker' pub, Gosford Street, *c.* 1919. The soldiers are presumably just home from the war.

Right: Westcotes Street party, one of many to celebrate the end of the Second World War. Note the other photographer centre right.

Below: A postcard depicting a decontamination unit of the period around the Second World War. Units like these reflected the widespread fear of gas attacks.

Left: Frances Watkins *née* Russell in what is thought to be her twenty-first birthday photograph in 1901.

Below: The back of the photograph of Frances Russell advertising the photographer Mr H. Gough's use of 'electric light'. His studio was described as an 'electric and daylight studio'.

Right: Claudia Russell, *c.* 1920.

Below: Claudia and some friends record a holiday
to Blackpool with a photographic postcard, *c.* 1920.

Left: Hilda Dalton, aged six in 1910.

Below: Coach and pair belonging to the Causers. They owned the Malt Shovel in Spon End from 1871 to 1926 and ran an undertaker's and taxi business from there. They also had premises in Swan Lane, which was where this photograph was taken.

Three youngsters clearly enjoying themselves despite the bare surroundings at the Meadow Street/
Trafalgar Street junction, *c.* 1959. The girl on the left is Julia Ward who attended Spon Street School,
with possibly her sister next to her.

Members of the Coventry and Midland Photographic Society, *c.* 1885. From left to right, standing: -?-, ? Banks, -?-, C. Ambrose, T. Owen, -?-. Seated: -?-, T.J. Lloyd, E.J. Walker, -?-.

The location of this shot of the Coventry Clarion Cycling Club is not known but it is possibly the Coat of Arms Bridge Road. It cannot be too far from Coventry, with the small children present. It was taken on 28 September 1913.

Cycling was a craze in the late nineteenth and early twentieth century. This group is from the Barras Green WMC in 1926.

Another Barras Green group but not a hat in sight in this later photograph.

Opposite: Ernie Slaymaker and Alf Pails in their Second World War Civil Defence uniforms. Ernie and Alf were part of the Civil Defence unit responsible for the Sir Thomas Whites Road area.

Right: Elsie Siddle visits the 'coal hole' during the war.

Singer

Alfred (72) and Gladys (71), of 68, Nunts Park Avenue, Holbrooks, Coventry, moved to the city from South Wales in 1929.

Mr. Wiggins has made a name for himself in churches throughout the city as a fine baritone singer. At one time he was a member of the BBC Midlands Chorus.

He still has an interest in music, and conducts a small group of singers called The Occasionals who sing at clubs and homes for old folk.

Alfred Wiggins (1902-76), a well-known Coventry soloist.

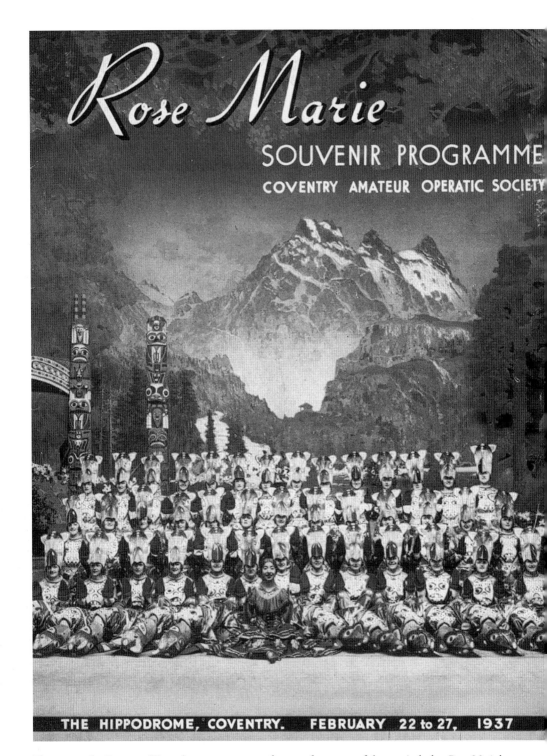

Rose Marie

SOUVENIR PROGRAMME

COVENTRY AMATEUR OPERATIC SOCIETY

THE HIPPODROME, COVENTRY. FEBRUARY 22 to 27, 1937

The cover of a Coventry Hippodrome programme for a performance of the musical play *Rose Marie* by the Coventry Amateur Operatic Society in 1937. It is described inside as 'a romance of the Canadian Rockies', and was performed for six nights and a Saturday matinee.

Mrs Edith Bagley displaying 1920s fashion. Born in Cow Lane, she moved to 'Munition Cottages' in Holbrooks when they were taken over by the Corporation from White & Poppe.

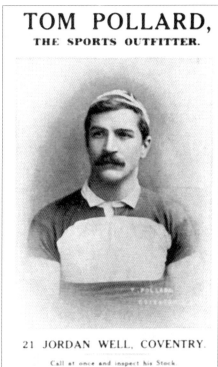

TOM POLLARD,
THE SPORTS OUTFITTER.

21 JORDAN WELL, COVENTRY.

Call at once and inspect his Stock.

Tom Pollard in his Coventry rugby union outfit. His shop, which used to be in Jordan Well opposite the Gaumont buildings was taken over by C.G. Davies who moved to Far Gosford Street and then Smithford Way.

SMALL HEATH HARRIERS - COVENTRY BRANCH
HEAD QUARTERS ALBANY HOTEL - 1912-13

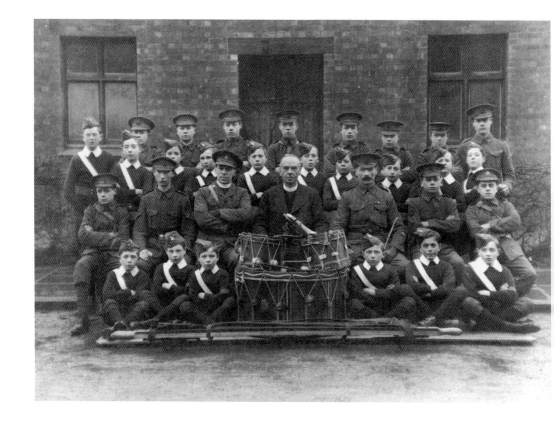

A well-dressed group outside the Gosford pub in St Georges Road. E.W. Dennis is seated front row, third from left and Bob Golding is fifth from left.

Opposite above: Small Heath Harriers, Coventry branch, outside their headquarters, the Albany Hotel, Albany Road, *c.* 1912-13. Mr Duffy is fifth from right in the centre row.

Opposite below: A Church Lads' Brigade group from 1916, outside St Chad's church on Stratford Street. In the centre are the Revd F. Reade and the Revd Hyslopp.

Above: One wonders whether the concoctions advertised could possibly live up to the claims made. The Sellors came from Derbyshire and were related to the Weltons, also chemists in Coventry.

Below: Is this the longest-trading company in the city? Astleys was founded in Coventry in 1730/31 as a chandler and dyesalter, their main products being oils, rope, canvas products and, as advertised here, agricultural seeds. Astleys was responsible, in 1998, for the restoration of the golden elephant in Broadgate, a local landmark.

Above and below: Two of the Civil Defence groups who did sterling work during the war. The state of the houses in the upper photograph underlines the dangerous nature of this work.

Above: Staff and trustees of Coventry Workhouse outside the old Whitefriars monastery building. This was the last building used for the workhouse inhabitants until it closed in 1943.

Left: Ann Russell (1838-1923). This photograph was taken around 1912. Ann is also shown on page 47, seated to the left of the bride Frances Russell, her daughter.

Right: Greyfriars Gate, taken down in 1784. This was the outlet to the south, standing roughly on the present Greyfriars Green.

Below: 'Whythburn', 14 The Terrace, Earlsdon Avenue South. Home and workplace of Robert Waddington Snr, a watchmaker, seen here presumably with his wife and daughter, *c.* 1910.

Above and below: Two productions from the St Barbara's Amateur Operatic Society's repertoire *Ali Baba*, below. Both productions took place during the 1920s and are photographed outside the church in Palmerston Road, Earlsdon.

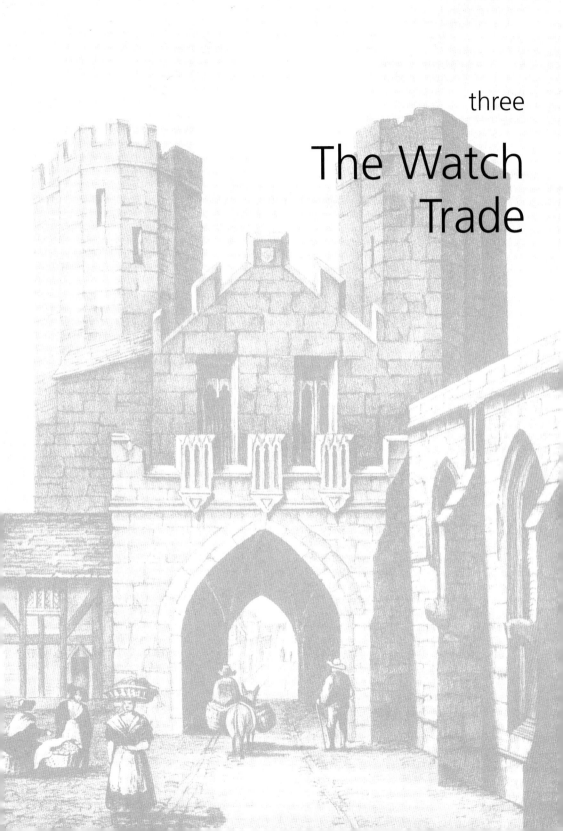

three

The Watch Trade

Left and below left: Joseph White (1835–1906) and his wife Catherine *née* Steane (1837–1904). Joseph was a watchmaker and industrialist. He joined Coventry Machinists in 1881 as Managing Director and also financially backed his son Alfred, the White in the White & Poppe engine business.

Below right: One of Joseph's highly accurate timepieces with a six-minute flying tourbillon movement. *(Courtesy of Sotheby's.)*

Above and below: The movement and component items of one of Joseph's productions.

Joseph Lee (1851–1908), apprenticed as a watch
engraver and then followed that trade. He lived
with his family in the Poddy Croft area and
presumably worked in the local Spon Street watch
industry.

Joseph's wife Sophia Maria Lee *née* Lomas (1854–
1915), *c.* 1902.

This cross, in silver, is an example of Joseph's engraving skills.

Spon Gate, near St John's church, viewed from Fleet Street. This gate, perhaps the most impressive of them all, led to Spon Street and Spon End, and was the main western access to the city. This area became a centre of the watch trade in the nineteenth century.

A drawing of 'Earlsdon House', the first to be built in Earlsdon Street. The house was originally built in 1852 for John Flinn, a watch manufacturer, with a watch factory at the rear. He also had built thirteen cottages in nearby Arden Street for his workers. The house, factory and cottages were bought by Joseph White in 1868, and he remained there until his death in 1906. This drawing depicts the house before Coventry Gauge & Tool Co. added offices to the front in 1935.

Opposite above: Known as the 'Bates house' after its owner Henry Bates, this house opposite Providence Street was the third built in Earlsdon Street at a cost of £87, plus £25 for plot 151, in 1852.

Opposite below: Situated in Earlsdon Avenue South, 'Woodlands' was built for the watch-case maker James Walker around 1855. He lived there for over fifty years until his death in 1907.

Samuel Yeomans,

WHOLESALE

WATCH MANUFACTURER,

Spon Street,

→✳ COVENTRY. ✳←

Gold and Silver English Lever Watches

OF EVERY DESCRIPTION.

PRICE LIST ON APPLICATION.

THREE-QUARTER PLATE, KEYLESS, CENTRE-SECONDS STOP WATCHES OF EVERY DESCRIPTION, FOR HOME AND EXPORT.

Samuel Yeomans was also in partnership with Isaac Jabez Theo Newsome and employed many apprentices in his workshops. This advertisement from 1890 shows the wide range of products which he had to offer.

Watchmaker Charles Corelli Johnson.

Above: Watch-case makers Henry and Mariah Robinson with their family. From left to right: Harry, Jack, Hannah, George, Elizabeth, Sarah, Arthur and Frank.

Right: J. West stands proudly outside his watchmaker and repairer shop at 27 Earlsdon Street, *c.* 1915.

An image of houses in Meadow Street/Trafalgar Street area showing the much larger windows installed for the 'top shops' – the large workshops which were one of the most distinctive features of the Coventry landscape prior to the clearances which occurred for the ring road development. Part of the old Rudge works are seen in the background to the right.

CHAPEL FIELDS,

Coventry, 18

M

Dr. to MRS. JANE DALTON,

ENGRAVER.

A blank invoice form from 1861. Thomas Dalton was apprenticed as a watch engraver in Spon End and started his own business after completing his indentures.

four

Schooldays

A girls class from St John's School, *c.* 1894. Ada Scrivener is in the back row, second from the left.

Wheatley Street School class five, with Claudia Russell in the front row, second from the right, *c.* 1902.

Right: Spon Gate, which was taken down in 1770, viewed from Spon Street. To the left of this viewpoint was the Fairfax Charity School, which was absorbed into Bablake School.

Below: A girls class of 1904 from St John's School. Ada Scrivener is in the back row on the right. Ada was a pupil at this school but is here a 'pupil teacher'.

A pupil teacher 'passing out' photograph with Ada Scrivener seated in the middle row, third from the left, *c.* 1907.

A class at Radford School, *c.* 1927. Mary Leeson, aged eight, with long hair in ringlets, is seated in the centre row on the right of the fourth desk from the front.

A photograph taken from *Coventry (Illustrated) Up-To-Date*, of the Wheatley Road Board School, *c.* 1896.

This beautifully illustrated certificate congratulates Claudia Russell for her perfect attendance at Wheatley Street Girls School in the year 1907/8. The certificate is decorated with various scenes from around Coventry, the arms of the city and cipher of the Coventry Education Committee.

Above and below: Two classes from Earlsdon School. The one above is from around 1927, with Mrs Betty Astill, who supplied the photograph, seated second from left at the desk in front.

Above: A class from Whoberley School, *c.* 1947. The lad seated on the right, third row from front, is the late Ken Siddle who was Chairman of P&O for two years in the 1980s.

Below: A Whoberley School soccer team, *c.* 1948. Tile Hill Lane houses are in the background. The teachers are Hubert Thomas (left), Mr Smith the Headmaster (centre) and Mr Day (right).

Whoberley School, Miss Jean's class of 1949. From left to right, back row: M Phillamore, J. Easthope, J. Stoppard, P. Flick, V. Payne, F. Jones, E. Beasley, A. Powel, E. Powel, B. Hanney. Middle row: I. Muir, J. Jones, P. Prothero, M. Hughes, K. Bailey, J. Smith, A. Stanger, F. Brewer, M. Howes, J. Wright, S. Roberts. Front row: P. Wilks, S. Plattern, J. Williams, P. Holdstock, K. Sedgley, C. Drayne, K. Cole, M. Jones, D. Radmall, F. Morgan, C. Greenway.

The first Earlsdon purpose-built schoolhouse, c. 1890. Prior to this, schooling had taken place in an old weaving shed in the village. This building soon became too small and a larger school had to be built.

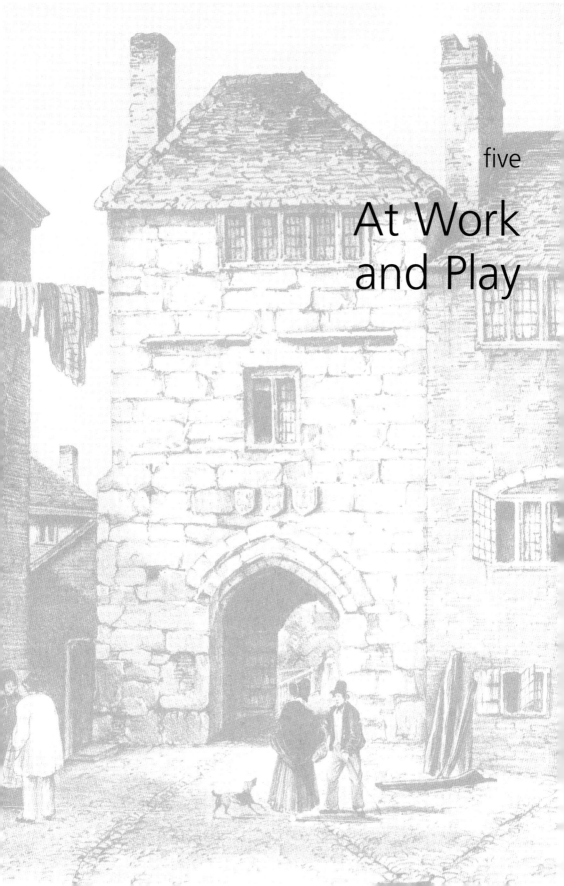

five

At Work
and Play

Sam Pails with his new bread delivery cart, *c.* 1920. Although the bakery is in Craven Street this photograph does not appear to have been taken in that area.

Old machinery, Meadow Street area, *c.* 1959. These would have been driven by an overhead belting system (see page 94). The machine to the right looks to be an early model of a metal turning lathe.

Right: Boiler house chimney with the Hood Street factory at rear. These were part of the original Humber cycle works (see page 32).

Below: This factory, in Alma Street, was used by Dunlop, whose signage can just be made out on the end wall. This building had its own well which was still open, but disused, in 1965. Read Street factory is at back.

Above: Inside the Coventry Gauge & Tool Co. factory in Earlsdon. Looking at the wooden flooring, this is possibly part of the original Flinn watch shops behind Earlsdon House.

Left: One of the company's products, modified with the addition of electric motors to replace overhead belt drive.

Leaving time at the Daimler works in Sandy Lane, pre-1914.

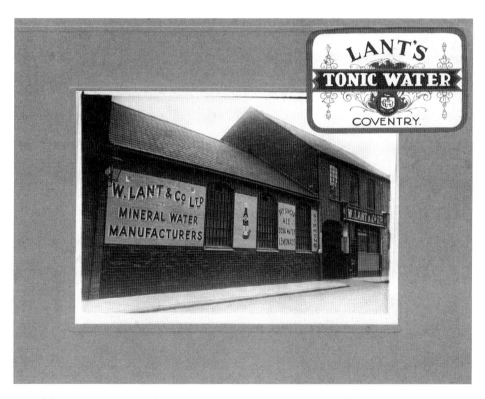

Part of the W. Lant & Co. Ltd bottling plant in Bond Street, plus one of their labels.

The Imperial picture house in Earlsdon Street and below, after conversion in 1951 to La Continentale which then specialised in European films.

Above: The interior of La Continentale.

Right: Mill Lane Gate, also called the Bastille Gate. This was sited between the Gosford and Swanswell Gates, being pedestrian access from what became Cox Street.

Coventry Fire Service float in the 1907 carnival. This was a Godiva Procession.

A carnival entry from the active Barras Green WMC.

The Barras Green WMC fishing section entry from the same year.

A 1956 carnival entry from the BTH Apprentices Training Dept, aided by a few friendly girls and the foreman, with the theme of the Romans conquering the ancient Britons.

One of the machining shops at the Standard works in Cashs Lane, *c.* 1923. The bars on the floor look like half-shaft blanks that are being produced by W.J. Ward on the machine front left.

A colour advertising card for S. Peters & Son Ltd removal firm, *c.* 1910. The business was based at 6 Ford Street.

The All Souls stoolball team from 1935. Stoolball is a game formerly common in England, especially with young women.

BTH Apprentices football team, 1954. From left to right, standing: trainer, -?-, B. Chivers, -?-, -?-, G. Barwick, -?-, D. Cockshutt, referee. Seated: B. Mace, A. Ross, J. Siddle, W. Shields, -?-.

Jack Harnott's popular band, *c.* 1922. Based in Coventry, they used to play at the Kings Head Hotel as well as other venues in the city and around Warwickshire.

St Barbara's Amateur Operatic Society orchestra, with the Clarke twins, Aubrey on violin, back row left, his brother Howard on cello, front row left, *c.* 1928.

COVENTRY'S SKATING RENDEZVOUS

THE REGENT ROLLERDROME.
ALBANY ROAD, COVENTRY

PHONE
COVENTRY 4997

3 SESSIONS DAILY
SUNDAYS AT 8 P.M.

This building was situated alongside the rail embankment with access from the bottom of Broomfield Road. At this time it was a rollerdrome, but it later became a popular dance hall which eventually burnt down in the 1960s.

Club swinging was a recognised healthy pastime for young ladies in the 1920s. This group from St Barbara's church in Palmerston Road no doubt enjoyed participating in the many competitions held in the city.

Canley Youth Club football team for 1956/57. From left to right, back row: Mr Mansfield, Geoff Barwick, Malcolm West, Jack Tregartha, Trevor Radcliffe, -?-, William Siddle, Tom Williams. Front row: -?-, -?-, Jack Siddle, Cyril West, -?-.

Cycle speedway groups were all around the town after the Second World War, this one was from Canley.

The Rex engine test room, pre-1913. Possibly the 'Nail Factory' in Moor Street before the move to premises in Osborne Road.

Charles Dalton and his brother Samuel aboard a 1907 experimental Rex car no. 16. This photograph was taken in the 'slang' alongside his mother's farmhouse in Benton Green Lane, Berkswell.

Off on holiday, mid-1950s style. This Armstrong Whitworth Argosy freighter of Silver City Airways took three cars, or two cars and a motorcycle combination on this flight, plus passengers. Flying from Lydd (Kent) to Le Touquet, this was the alternative to a Channel ferry crossing. Although cars were driven into the hold, motorcycles had to be pushed in!

six

Transport

Workers pose for a photograph during the construction of Lockhurst Lane Bridge by Kelly & Sons of Foleshill in 1930. Albert Horner is second from left. Bert cycled from Liverpool looking for steady work, and he obviously found it, as he settled his family in Stretton and later in Coventry, working at the Ordnance in Red Lane for many years.

Right: Gosford Gate, which was built in the second half of the fourteenth century, overlooking the ancient crossing of the Sherbourne. It was taken down in 1765. The gate was the entrance to the city from the east. In the nineteenth century Gosford Street was the home of a few motor factories, of which the White & Poppe engine factory and Calcott car factory are still in use.

Below: A 1920s view of the corner of Hearsall Common, with the commemorative drinking fountain and horse trough on their original site.

Some Clarion Cycling Club members, still in the age when the wearing of headgear was considered part of being properly dressed. The *Clarion* was the news sheet of the SDP (see page 25).

An Anglo American Oil Co. Ltd delivery vehicle, *c.* 1905.

An Anglo-American tank wagon used in a procession to honour fallen servicemen, *c.* 1920. Driver C. Neilson is holding the horse.

In this later photograph driver C. Neilson has changed jobs and has updated to a petrol-driven lorry.

Left: Hilda Dalton on her bicycle, *c.* 1920. Highland Road is in the background.

Below: Mrs Henry Welton *née* Sellors at the tiller of a steam-driven car made by the Stanley Motor Carriage Co. of the USA, *c.* 1902.

Opposite below: Mortons Ltd operated in Coventry for many years. Note the driver's high seat. A cart with this load would have needed a team of horses to pull it effectively.

Above: Pony and trap and a handcart, both used for deliveries in the late nineteenth century, outside the Earlsdon Stores off-licence on Cromwell Street.

Two sizes of steam roller, a common sight at road works up to 1950. These are at work at the Earlsdon crossroads at the end of the nineteenth century.

A new railway bridge was necessary when Albany Road was built. The old bridge structure is still visible in this photograph taken around 1896.

A rail accident at Albany Road in 1904. Temporary tracks were laid to haul the coaches back up the embankment onto the line.

'Railway cottages' in Warwick Road. Built to house railway workers in the nineteenth century, they were situated between King Henry VIII School and the embankment and were demolished around 1970.

This image shows an early monoplane piloted by Bentfield C. Hucks. Benny Hucks was the first Englishman to fly a loop-the-loop, and he became known as 'the upside down aviator'. He is shown here during a display in July 1913 in Coventry, in his seventy horsepower tandem Bleriot military-type monoplane.

A 1923 omnibus with a difference: this was a BTH prototype with a petrol-electric propulsion system. It was entered in a 1,000-mile vehicle trial around the country, which it completed satisfactorily, but its high initial cost and weight caused further development to be abandoned.

The solid tyres on this fully laden charabanc must have delivered an uncomfortable ride for these 1920s workers on a day out.

Ford Model T truck used for a carnival float by the Barras Green WMC in 1925.

A postcard advertising the Rover twelve horsepower car, *c.* 1912.

Charles Dalton and family on his Rex combination in 1914, note the warning device for passenger use! The engine was possibly of the type shown on page 105.

Construction of roads and sewers for the Cheylesmore estate in 1935 by A. Robinson contractors.

An outing from the Rover works, *c.* 1924. Bantam Coaches operated from the Spon End arches for many years before being absorbed into Red House Motors.

Coventry Transport buses were registered with their fleet number. This 1930s Daimler is still without the 'Coventry' on the cream centre band.

A 'Bottle Car', used for advertising and based on a Daimler car chassis. They were seen in some carnival processions.

A tram leaving Broadgate. In background left is the New Hippodrome with the old Hippodrome still standing on its right.

Above and below: Two 1929 carnival entries from the Alvis 'Motor Touring Club'.

Above: A 1934 front entrance double-decker bus. This was built by English Electric for the Birmingham & Midland Motor Omnibus Co. Ltd (known to all as Midland Red). HA9432 was written on the back of the photograph.

Right: The Coventry Garages were at the Spon Street end of the Holyhead Road, they later sold Rootes Group products from this site.

Standard Flying 12, 1936, from a painting by C.S. Gibberd.

An early two-tone Standard Vanguard. The roof line is similar to the car above which itself echoed the lines of the 1933 Riley Kestrel 9.

ERA of 1935 from a sketch by C.S. Gibberd. Although produced at Bourne in Lincolnshire, they used modified Riley 1.5-litre 6-cylinder racing engines and the gearboxes were Wilson pre-selector units made by Armstrong Siddeley at Parkside.

Reproduction of a montage 'Jaguar at Le Mans' (© Solomon & Whitehead), by
Coventry artist Graham Bosworth. Now that car production is finishing at Browns
Lane, it is worth noting that of the cars shown, apart from the 'Silk Cut', No 44

and the white E-types which were privately developed, the rest were produced at Browns Lane by the Competitions Department.

Other local titles published by Tempus

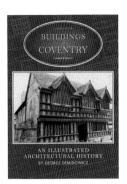

Buildings of Coventry

GEORGE DEMIDOWICZ

The buildings featured cover almost a millennium of Coventry's history. There are one thousand statutory and locally listed buildings in the city and many of these are splendid examples of their period. This book describes and illustrates some of the finest examples that can be seen today and will serve as a useful guide for those wishing to explore and learn more about the city's history through its buildings.

07524 3115 3

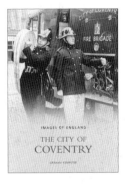

The City of Coventry

GRAHAM KEMPSTER

This collection of 170 archive photographs is drawn from the archives of the *Coventry Evening Telegraph*, the local daily newspaper which has served the people of Coventry since 1891. They highlight some of the important events that have occurred in the city during the last century, including blitz bombing during the Second World War, and the arrival of the railway at the end of the nineteenth century.

07524 3357 1

Coventry City Football Club 100 Greats

GEORGE ROWLAND

Over 6,000 players have proudly worn the colours of Coventry City since the club was formed as Singers FC in 1883. This volume offers a retrospective look at 100 of the finest players to have represented the club, with a detailed examination of their time at Coventry and their careers in football. As a biographical and statistical reference guide to Coventry's greatest players, this volume is second to none. As an enjoyable wander down memory lane, it is a must for all followers of the Sky Blues.

07524 2294 4

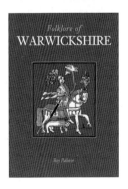

Folklore of Warwickshire

ROY PALMER

Situated at the very heart of England, Warwickshire is a county steeped in tradition, folklore and mythology. Revised from the original, this new illustrated edition is a fascinating study of folklore rooted firmly within the context of popular culture and history. There are tales of saints and sinners, sports and pastimes, fairs and wakes, folk songs and balladry, including many musical examples, as well as the passage rites of birth, marriage and death.

07524 3359 8

If you are interested in purchasing other books published by Tempus, or in case you have difficulty finding any Tempus books in your local bookshop, you can also place orders directly through our website

www.tempus-publishing.com